W9-BFQ-155

PERFECT BALANCE

PERFECT BALANCE

THE STORY OF AN ELITE GYMNAST

by

LYNN HANEY

photographs by

BRUCE CURTIS

G.P. PUTNAM'S SONS   NEW YORK

Text copyright © 1979 by Lynn Haney
Illustrations copyright © 1979 by Bruce Curtis
All rights reserved.
Published simultaneously in Canada by
Longman Canada Limited, Toronto.
Printed in the United States of America
Book design by Kathleen Westray
Library of Congress Cataloging in Publication Data
Haney, Lynn. Perfect balance.
Summary: Follows the career of a young American
gymnast as she prepares for the 1980 Olympics to be
held in Moscow. Includes profiles of several other
prominent figures in gymnastic competition.
1. Russo, Leslie—Juvenile literature.
2. Gymnasts—United States—Biography—Juvenile
literature. 3. Gymnastics—Juvenile literature.
[1. Russo, Leslie. 2. Gymnasts. 3. Gymnastics]
I. Curtis, Bruce. II. Title.
GV460.2.R87H36 796.4′1′0924 [B] [92] 78-11634
ISBN 0-399-20661-2

Third Impression

6704

ACKNOWLEDGMENTS

We are indebted to many individuals for their assistance in the preparation of this book. Muriel Grossfeld, George Ward, Mike and Ina Russo, Ben and Valerie Cassello, Chris and Charlie Frederick, as well as Frank Bare, executive director of the United States Gymnastics Federation, all contributed time and valuable information to the project. Special thanks to our editor, Margaret Frith, and to Diane Bidermann, whose photograph appears on the back of the jacket.

NOBODY ever dreamed that Leslie Russo would grow up to be an athlete, a graceful, disciplined perfectionist, with a fierce, competitive spirit.

Leslie started out as a fluff ball. She never climbed trees with her older sister, Valerie. She squirmed as she watched Val catch tadpoles in the freshwater pond near their house in Newington, Connecticut. And in the summer, when the Russos went to the shore, Leslie had to be dragged to the beach. She didn't like the sand. She sat cross-legged on a blanket, under the shade of a striped umbrella, watching Val and their two brothers, Mike and Tony, make sand castles.

At age fifteen, Leslie is an elite gymnast, one of a small number of young women who have attained the highest level of classification in the sport.

She is still feminine and graceful, with smooth olive skin, soft brown eyes, and a gentle smile. She is five feet tall. Her ninety-three pounds are perfectly proportioned.

The only clue to the life she leads is in her hands. Calluses, hard as a lumberjack's, run across her palms. These are the price she pays for hours spent swinging monkey-style from uneven bars, one of four major events in gymnastics.

Leslie, a sophomore at Coginchaug High, goes to school from 8:00 A.M. to 12:30 P.M. Then she puts on her leotard and spends six arduous hours in a gym with a single goal in mind—to be one of the six American women gymnasts to compete in the 1980 Olympics in Moscow. "I'm determined to go to Russia," she says, "and win a gold medal for the United States."

Leslie has a good chance of making it to the 1980 Olympics, which means that every time she faces a major competition it is both exhilarating and a cliff-hanger. Each meet brings her that much closer or that much further from her goal. "She's in the top ten in the country now, and every day she gets better," says head elite coach Don Peters at Grossfeld's Gymnastics Center where Leslie trains.

When Leslie was six, her mother enrolled her in Donna Paretti's dancing school in Newington, where she took baton, tap, ballet, and acrobatics. "Right away you knew she was exceptional," says Donna Paretti. Even then, Leslie was strong and extremely flexible. She had a good back and straight legs. She also showed a capacity to work hard. Acrobatics was Leslie's special talent. After a few years when Leslie was older, Donna suggested to Mrs. Russo that Leslie take up gymnastics.

Her mother took her to a gymnastics class in West Hartford conducted by a seasoned pro named Gay Amado. The coach put Leslie through a series of elementary tumbling routines and then turned to her mother and said, "She is going to be an Olympic star. I don't want to touch her. I want you to take her to Muriel Grossfeld. She's the best women's gymnastics coach in the country."

Mrs. Russo said, "You've got to be kidding. How can you say that ten years from now Leslie will be an Olympian?"

"I'm not kidding you," said Gay Amado. "I've had this school for many years. I know the good ones. I know the mediocre ones. Leslie has the style, the grace, and the beauty of a champion gymnast. What more do you want?"

When Leslie heard about Muriel's school, she said, "I'm going tomorrow."

So Leslie, at age nine, became a pupil of Muriel Grossfeld, a legendary figure in the world of gymnastics.

As a child, Muriel was so sturdy that she won bets by reading whole comic books standing on her head. Three times she competed for the United States in the Olympics—at Melbourne, Rome, and Tokyo. Twice she was the U.S. women's Olympic Coach—in Mexico City and Munich.

When Leslie started training with her, Muriel's gym was in what once had been an A & P store in New Haven, Connecticut. The ceiling was so low that Muriel had holes cut out above the uneven bars and the vaulting horse so her students could work out without smashing an overhead light.

Muriel placed Leslie in a special class of eighteen students who appeared to have talent. They met twice a week, on Mondays and Fridays.

"Leslie stood out because she had a faster learning rate than the other gymnasts," says Muriel. "Also, she has charisma—that attention-getting thing which draws eyes to her. Everybody who was in the gym would notice what she was doing."

Muriel started Leslie doing forward rolls, smooth 360-degree rolls starting on the hands and ending on the feet. Soon Leslie could do handstands, backbends, and front limbers. (Front limbers are elegant, fluid movements—a combination of handstands and backbends.)

"Leslie is very catlike," says Muriel. "You know the stories about how if a cat falls, it twists and somersaults and spins to land on its feet. Leslie has that quality. She knows where she is in space."

With Muriel Grossfeld

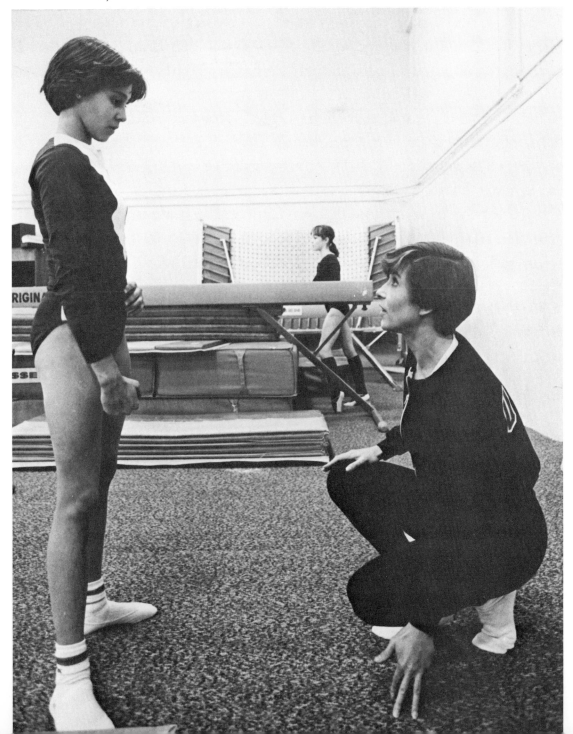

Next Muriel started teaching Leslie the four basic gymnastic events in which she would compete: uneven bars, vaulting, balance beam, and floor exercise. In competition, she would have to perform two routines in each event: "compulsaries," a set of movements that are the same for every gymnast, and "optionals," a set of free movements that are different for each gymnast.

UNEVEN BARS

THIS is the newest of the events in women's competition and among the most spectacular. At first, the gymnast might grip the lower bar, which is about back height, swing one leg up and pull her body up and around the bar. Later she learns to keep up a continuous movement in and out of the two bars. She will transfer from bar to bar with "kips," casting movements, turns, and jumps and, like a propeller, pivot around the bar. A complete routine, at Leslie's elite level, is likely to consist of twelve to eighteen different movements, usually performed in less than a minute.

For competition Leslie goes through a special procedure. "You don't have time on a kip to say, 'Toes on bar, thrust my feet, pull'—all the things that are going on in the routine—because it is so quick," says Leslie. "Before you start, you play over your whole bar routine in your mind, real fast. Then you wipe your mind blank. You walk up to the apparatus and look at it. You say to yourself, 'Okay, I'm going to jump in.' Then, once you begin, you don't hear anything because you're concentrating so hard."

VAULTING

VAULTING is one of the earliest and most natural gymnastic movements. It involves the body "flying" through space before and after contacting the "horse." This piece of equipment may have originated with the knights in the Middle Ages. Gymnasts used to vault with a horse that had a fake head and tail attached to it.

The gymnast begins with an approach run to the vault in which she creates momentum. Then she flies from a reuther board, which is the board from which the gymnast bounces, and lands on her hands on the horse. The second flight phase, called the afterflight, refers to the space of time after the hands leave contact with the horse and before the feet touch the floor.

Aside from amplitude, the height or range of her flight, particularly in the second phase, the gymnast is scored on the particular vault she's selected. For example, if she chooses a handspring with a full twist on the afterflight, the judges will look to see if she did the twist at the height of her flight, that she finished her twist, and that she had good form, particularly straight legs and pointed toes.

A good vaulter must be able to run quickly and jump for the springboard aggressively.

One of Muriel's students is Jackie Cassello, only twelve, the top junior vaulting champion in the United States. Jackie's willingness to conquer fear is a great advantage in vaulting. When you run down the vaulting runway, you must run as fast as you can, and you are virtually out of control. "Once you commit to the violence of the run, you are committing to the entirety," says Muriel. "That's why most kids slow down. They want to do the trick but they're scared of it or they want to think about it as they hit the board. A natural vaulter really desires to get to that point of being eight feet in the air turning over. Jackie Cassello enjoys the results. The higher the better as far as she is concerned."

In the last five years, vaulting for girls has become much more exciting and difficult than ever before in the history of the sport. Due to equipment improvements, and rule changes, really dramatic somersault vaults started showing up in women's gymnastics in 1973 and 1974.

Jackie Cassello does a vault called the Tsukahara, a back somersault from her hands to the floor in a straight body position, which was first seen in the Montreal Olympics in 1976, performed by Soviet gymnast Nelli Kim.

Jackie Cassello

BALANCE BEAM

FROM the start, beam was Leslie's best event. The challenge is to demonstrate maximum range of motion on a cushioned plank that is approximately sixteen feet long and four inches wide.

The event is increasingly becoming more exacting and thrilling because of the tremendously difficult tumbling stunts (flip-flops, aerial cartwheels and walkovers, back somersaults) being attempted by the gymnasts. Movements must be completed between one minute fifteen seconds and one minute thirty-five seconds.

"What is so difficult about the balance beam," says Muriel, "is that you must be thinking about everything you are doing every second. Most of the hours my students spend practicing are not to learn the tricks but to know how to perform the exercises under the unbelievable stress of competition.

"Leslie's beam is special because of the quality of movement. There's an old saying that judges have: 'A truly great balance beam would look like it was on the floor.' She comes the closest of any present competitor in the world right now to achieving that description. Most gymnasts are much too safe and exact, militaristic in this approach to beam. Leslie works with an abandon and freedom of rhythm that most people aren't willing to do. Her beam is totally soft and lyrical."

FLOOR exercise is a mix of ballet, modern dance, tumbling, handsprings, and other skills. It is performed within approximately a forty-foot square, with a time limit of one to one and a half minutes, and it is always accompanied by music. Floor exercise is Muriel's specialty and she strives to develop a routine for each gymnast which reflects the girl's personality. "I have a pride about not wanting my gymnasts to look as if they come out of the same choreographer's factory," says Muriel.

For Leslie, Muriel devised a floor exercise that is a heady mixture of Spanish dancing and the soft, mysterious music used in the desert scenes in the movie *Lawrence of Arabia.* "Leslie has a wonderful lyrical quality and the whole routine is built around that," says Muriel. "You get the feeling that she is in a vast desert and she gallops and she gallops and she gallops."

A coach must have a fine eye, and Muriel saw that Leslie had the temperament to be a competitive gymnast. Leslie has a steady, even, generous disposition. She's cool under pressure and she bounces back after a defeat. And she loves gymnastics.

After a year, when Leslie was ten, Muriel promoted her to the junior team, which meant that she would now participate in gymnastics competitions.

The girl who has the greatest physical talent isn't always the one who makes the best gymnast. It takes great mental desire to work toward a goal, and Leslie has what it takes and more.

At home, while carrying on a conversation in the kitchen with her mother, Leslie often did backbends, twists, and flexed her muscles, all the while chattering about her friends.

Leslie has always been close to her sister Valerie, who is four years older. Val is a dancer and has some understanding of gymnastics tricks. After gym class at night, Leslie often said, "Hey Val. Come and watch me. Tell me how I'm doing. I want to know if I'm doing it right" or "I want to see if this looks good."

Olga Korbut

In the basement of their Newington house, the Russos had a practice mat. Leslie and Valerie spent many evening hours practicing routines—front walkovers, back walkovers, tumbling, dancing.

"I wanted her to be the best because she's my sister," Valerie remembers. "Sometimes I'd make her cry until she hit a trick. She'd go running upstairs and Mother would say, 'What did you do to her?' I'd say, 'She's going to do it right if it kills me.' But, anyway, Leslie wanted to do the best she could. She's a perfectionist."

Leslie had been training with Muriel for a year when the 1972 Olympics appeared on television. Like many other young girls, Leslie was profoundly influenced by Olga Korbut, the little pixie from Grodno, USSR, with her blond hair in yarn-tied pigtails, who enchanted the entire world.

Olga became the most recognized female name and face in the world. For the first time in the history of sports a woman athlete had become a global star. Cathy Rigby set off sparks when she won a silver medal on the beam for the United States at the World Games in 1971, but Olga made millions of people aware of gymnastics.

Olga was the Pied Piper of the sport, the picture of vibrant, impetuous youth. Her most intriguing event was the floor exercise, in which she dazzled the crowd with her leaps and acrobatic tricks.

In her floor routine Olga imitated ants, butterflies, grasshoppers—all the while laughing, pouting, grimacing, and teasing. She looked just like a little kid saying to the crowd, "Come gym with me. This is terrific fun." When she landed on her stomach in a back somersault, the audience was in ecstasy.

"When I saw Olga on TV," said Leslie, "I thought, Wow, I want to do that. I want to try harder stuff. I want to be like her, a winner, but do it my way. Not copy her style."

As a result of Olga's appeal, interest in gymnastics exploded in the United States. Before 1970, there were only about five or six good programs for gymnasts scattered throughout the country. Today, some 200,000 American women are competing in the sport, and that figure does not include the tens of thousands of aspiring gymnasts who have not yet reached a competitive level.

When Leslie turned eleven she started competing at local meets and she quickly stacked up a steady stream of firsts and seconds.

Val constantly encouraged Leslie. "I'd leave her little notes the night before a meet," says Val. "I'd say, 'Leslie, just concentrate. I know you're going to wow them.'"

But Leslie was shy and couldn't believe she had the natural talent to be a first-class athlete. If she pulled off a difficult trick at a meet, she didn't think she had done anything exceptional. "Don't make such a big thing about it," Leslie would tell her parents. "Anybody can do what I can do. I'm just ordinary."

Between her eleventh and twelfth birthdays, Leslie started having doubts about gymnastics. The hills were getting higher. "Every time I'd go to a meet, I'd see people doing harder combinations of tricks," says Leslie. The training was more rigorous and she was having to make more sacrifices, giving up almost all her free time. She saw that in order to be a champion, she had to dedicate herself to nonstop training.

If you want to be a champion, "You can't get out of shape for even a week and expect to keep improving," says Muriel. "Gymnastics becomes the center of your life." A lot of Leslie's friends from the gym had dropped out, deciding that the price was too high to pay. Leslie wanted to be with her friends.

She dreaded telling her father. He is a partner in a gravel contracting company in Hartford and for years he had been spending his spare time going to meets and cheering Leslie on. She was the apple of his eye and he wanted, almost more than anything, to have her excel in gymnastics.

One evening, after dinner, she was sitting alone with her father at the dinner table. She said, "Daddy, I want to quit."

"You do?"

"Daddy, I don't want to be an Olympian."

"Leslie, I don't care if you are an Olympian but give yourself a chance. Maybe you'll feel differently next week."

"I want to be like other girls. I want to go out and play tennis. I want to go swimming. I want to watch television. I don't want to be under pressure like this."

Her father talked to her for an hour. Finally he said, "I'm your father and I'm going to ask something of you. I'm going to ask you to stay in gymnastics for one more year. If at the end of the year you still feel like quitting, that's fine with me. No questions asked."

"Okay, Daddy," Leslie answered. "I'll do that."

In that year Leslie became the Connecticut Junior Gymnastics Champion, the Junior Regional Champion (a seven-state title), and, at twelve, she was the youngest contender in the national United States Gymnastics Federation (USGF) meet in Fairfax, Connecticut where she placed tenth among approximately one hundred contenders.

Just about the time Leslie was proving she had what it takes to be an international competitor, faulty wiring set off a fire on the first floor of the Russos' home. It was twelve thirty at night.

Leslie was sitting on the living room sofa finishing a homework assignment on Peru when she looked over and saw the curtains go up in flames, the house starting to fill with smoke. She ran downstairs to the cellar and scooped up three puppies, whelped by her Irish setter, Heather. She barely made her escape. By the time the fire engines arrived, the house was a stack of charred timbers.

With her father

The Russos bought another house in Durham, Connecticut. Even though the fire had dealt them a severe financial blow, they never considered pulling Leslie out of competitive gymnastics. Instead they did without rugs, curtains, and other things most people take for granted.

In addition to the cost of lessons, Leslie needed leotards and spending money. "I own about twenty leotards," says Leslie. Some get small. Others fade. They wear out after a while. "I hardly have any regular clothes because I spend so much time in leotards."

Mrs. Russo kept a green jar on her bureau in her bedroom, a piggybank to help further Leslie's career. "Every extra cent I get goes for Leslie," said Mrs. Russo. "Pennies, nickels, dimes, quarters. It adds up."

Leslie's brothers, Tony, twenty-four, and Mike, twenty-three, saw Mrs. Russo dropping coins into the jar and they started doing the same.

During Christmas week of 1976, Muriel opened a spacious new gym in Milford, Connecticut, and she was attracting top talent from all over the East Coast. Although Leslie continued to live at home, twelve of the girls stayed in a dorm next to the school. Leslie could see that things were getting more competitive.

The year before, Muriel hired Don Peters, a nationally known gymnastics figure, who gave up his own team, the Tumble Bees, in order to join Muriel as Grossfeld's head elite coach. His standards are just as high as Muriel's.

The girls start each day at the gym with warm-up routines. These exercises are done before practicing specific routines. Each part of the body should be gradually flexed so that muscles are ready for more strenuous movement.

Warm-ups are done to the piano accompaniment played by Peter Feigelman. Peter is a boisterous Russian who emigrated to the United States two years ago and settled in Waterbury, Connecticut. He was the third ranking piano player for the Soviet gymnastics team, playing for Olga Korbut and Ludmila Tourischeva. Of the girls at Muriel's Peter says, "They will be as good as the best Soviets. It's just a matter of time."

Peter introduced many enjoyable innovations into the stretch and side split warm-up routines, usually dull preliminary exercises that prepare the body for the hard work the muscles will be put through in the day.

To the hopping beat of show tunes, the girls run through ballet exercises, the cancan, the Charleston, and the cakewalk, which is a high-stepping strut dating back to the turn of the century.

Then the girls break up into groups and work with their respective coaches. Muriel teaches floor exercises and the balance beam. She is a trained dancer, and dancing plays a large part in these two events. She is also a relentless perfectionist. Says Muriel, "I'm known as the Great Dictator."

Muriel is in her thirties. Back in the 1950s and 1960s, she was an Olympic gymnast. In 1964, she achieved the highest score in gymnastics, the perfect 10, at the Olympic trials. She was then the only American woman to earn a 10 and, even now, Muriel is so flexible she can execute tricks on the balance beam that even her rubber-boned students can't do.

Head elite coach Don Peters

Don Peters trains the girls on bars and vaulting. Like Muriel, gymnastics is his life. "When I was little, I wanted to fly," says Don. "With gymnastics you can do that."

Two coaches, Rich Carlson and Andy Antoniolli, spot the girls as they go through vaulting and uneven bars. A spotter assists by supporting, lifting, or catching the gymnast as a stunt is being performed.

Spotting is crucial in gymnastics because it is a safeguard against injury. Also, when a gymnast begins to learn a trick, the spotter will help steer her through the movement until she develops a sense of orientation about it. For this reason the coach's role is more important than in other athletics and the relationship between student and teacher closer.

"A lot of girls get crushes on Richie," says Leslie. "Because he's fun and nutty. If you're in a rotten mood, he's the one in the gym who tries to cheer you up."

The girls spend three hours a day working on their "compulsories." Then they work on "optionals."

"Sometimes I get tired of the grind," says Leslie, "but those feelings don't last long. I love this. Particularly, if I warm up good. 'Ah,' I say to myself. 'This is going to be a good day today.' "

It takes enormous willpower and discipline to push your body to its natural limits every day. "Some days you just feel so bad that you don't like doing it at all but you have to do it," says Leslie. "You say to yourself, 'I can't do this. I'm too tired.' But when you go to a meet, you're glad you worked out those days. They pay off."

In good weather the girls run every day. They also do sprints and run backward. "In the driveway of the gym there's a little slant and we push cars up the driveway," says Leslie. "It builds up strength in your legs. A lot of people stop on the road. 'Oh, you need help?' They think the car is stalled."

With coach Rich Carlson

Weekends are Leslie's days of rest. In the winter she spends them
ice-skating or skiing. The rest of the year it's horseback riding or competing at
dog shows. Leslie has been showing Irish setters now for three years.

"Any dog shows this weekend?" Leslie asks her mother when Friday rolls
around. At the dog shows, in an entirely different environment, Leslie finds
relaxation from the constant demands of gymnastics.

"Karen Edwards, my best friend, lives next door," Leslie explains. "She and
I go to dog shows together. She has collies and I have setters. She also has
horses, and we ride together on the trails around Durham. And Karen likes
gymnastics too."

In the evenings, Leslie plays the piano to relax and, like Olga Korbut, she
reads mystery stories. Sometimes she becomes so absorbed in what she is
reading that she walks upstairs staring at the page of a book.

At thirteen, Leslie began preparing to advance from the junior division class to the elite level. To qualify as an elite, she would be judged by much more rigorous standards than she had ever known before. On the surface, Leslie's life seemed to be running smoothly but, in fact, she was going through a difficult time with gymnastics.

As Don and Muriel began teaching Leslie increasingly difficult tricks, they stressed development over winning. They saw that, particularly on balance beam, Leslie had a stunning future. So they began to accelerate her routines, especially on this event, replacing easy moves with difficult tricks.

On beginner level compulsories Leslie averaged 9.6 and 9.7, which is excellent for a student in the early stages of her career. But as Leslie attempted more difficult routines in competition, she sometimes failed, when, if she hadn't been trying such hard maneuvers, she would have succeeded.

ORIGINAL

"The thing that comes hard for Leslie is getting her mind to control her body," explains Muriel. "She feels her gymnastics more than she thinks her gymnastics. For example, on her balance beam routine, Leslie will be doing flip-flop backs just so high in the gym. She'll go into a meet and do one two feet higher. But she won't understand how to do the flip-flop back and then come down on the balance beam. For this reason, she sometimes fell when, if she'd used her head, she could have pulled it off."

When Leslie blows a routine she hits the side of her thigh and knocks her head. Then she'll say, "Oh, I stink."

"You don't stink," Don will say. "You just aren't using your head."

As summer slipped into fall and the time for Leslie's qualifying meet drew near, the tension in the gym stepped up. "Puttin' the clamps on" Muriel called it. But as Muriel and Don put Leslie through her routines, they were often forced to keep her late and work her on weekends because Leslie was rebelling against the pressure.

Leslie was frightened, and when this happens she becomes quietly stubborn, messing around, getting stuck on a particular part of her routine.

"I was having a problem doing a trick in my floor exercise," explains Leslie. "Muriel told me to do something and I couldn't do it and she started getting mad because I kept doing the same thing over and over and she thought I wasn't trying. That's when you get most discouraged. When you keep trying your best and you can't do it right. And your coach doesn't think you're trying."

"Coaches use different ways to get you to try a trick. Sometimes they will yell at you and you get so scared you have to do it. You're scared of them and you're scared of the trick and they make you overcome your fear. Or they dare you. They say, 'I betcha can't do it,' and you say, 'Yeah. I can.' And you do it."

After Leslie finished her floor exercise, she went to Don to practice vaulting. Don, like Muriel, sometimes loses patience with her. When Leslie muffed her vaulting, he yelled at her.

For some girls the coach's anger has a positive effect—it permits them to replace their fear with an anger of their own, freeing them to be more aggressive in their performance of the skill. "When you're afraid, you get more energy," says Leslie. But on that day, Leslie wasn't feeling secure enough to take criticism. She cried, retreating into herself, no longer sharing her feelings. She went home, upstairs to her bedroom, and didn't come out for hours. She thought, I'm no good. I can't do gymnastics anymore.

Leslie stayed away from the gym for two weeks and no amount of persuasion by the Russos or the staff at Grossfeld's could get her to return. Finally, Muriel and Don took Leslie out to dinner and talked to her, offering the kind of support she needed, the vote of confidence that meant so much because it was coming from her coaches.

"Leslie," Muriel urged, "you can't just pack in years of hard work. You're dynamite. You have so much ahead of you. You have great talent."

Leslie returned to the gym and started concentrating, trying to get her mind and her body to work as one.

At her first qualifying meet she didn't make it but the second time around, in Syracuse, New York, she not only qualified but scored an all-around total of 73 points, or at least 9.0 in each of eight events.

As an elite, Leslie qualified for the first USGF National Elite Gymnastics meet to be held in Princeton, New Jersey, in February, 1977. This meet represented the cream of the entire country's gymnastics talent. The top ten competitors would qualify for a chance to compete for the U.S. Women's National Team in a meet to be held in California in April of the year.

The thought of participating in such an important event brought back Leslie's old feelings of insecurity but now she felt more equipped to handle them.

Leslie went to Princeton.

It's hard to sleep the night before a meet and, as many gymnasts do, Leslie turns a movie camera on in her mind to psych herself up for the competition. "It's as if I'm floating above my body and watching myself run through each routine," says Leslie. "I say, 'Okay, vaulting.' Sometimes I think of a bad vault. Then I say, 'Wait. Now, do it over and do it right this time.' And then I try to do every routine perfect. Like on beam. I think of a routine without any bobbles in it. [A bobble is a wobble on a beam.] Now handspring mount, stretch, smooth, walk-ready for aerial, and so on.

"Then I say my prayers. I say, 'Dear God. I hope I can do really good in this meet and I hope everybody else can do their best.' "

Gymnastics is one of those rare sports in which grooming counts. It's not in the rule book, but femininity is part of the tradition of women's gymnastics. So just before a meet Leslie washes her hair and shaves her legs. "I put a little blusher on and a little eye shadow around my eyelids so I don't look blah."

When Leslie walked out onto the floor of Princeton University's Jadwin Gymnasium, she was one of the youngest gymnasts there and one of the tiniest. She looked around in disbelief and became very quiet, blending into the background.

"When I saw Kolleen Casey and Robin Huebner out there," Leslie recalls with a smile, "the only thing I could think was Wow! I couldn't believe I was there competing with them. It was a big thrill for me because I never thought I would be going up against people like that."

Only seven months before, Leslie had seen Kolleen Casey competing with Olga Korbut, Nadia Comaneci, and Nelli Kim at the Montreal Olympics.

Kolleen Casey was one of the most exciting gymnasts in the United States. In 1975 she won a gold medal at the Pan American Games in Mexico. In 1976, she traveled to Peking for the China-U.S.A. meet. Robin Huebner had also competed internationally, including meets in Japan and in the USSR. Leslie was troubled. "At first I thought I don't have a chance. They're all so good."

As she waited her turn, Leslie tried to keep her emotions under control. Those who can successfully cope with pressure are the ones who succeed in gymnastics. "You get so nervous," says Leslie. "You get scared and you think about all the people watching you. A lot of times you do a lot better in competition than in workouts because you're really scared. You're keyed up and you feel a lot stronger."

Soon it was Leslie's turn for the balance beam. Though normally this is her best event, it is always a cause for anxiety because it's harder to get a good score on beam. If you make a small bobble on the beam it is usually one-or-two-tenths of a point. A medium bobble will cost you two-tenths or three-tenths of a point and if you fall to the floor, you're out a point.

With the true grace of a champion, Leslie did a handspring onto the end of the beam, and then kept going, flying forward, pushing with her hands. She was the most graceful of the women performers, spinning, turning and jumping, tumbling backward in a flip-flop, making the most difficult tricks seem effortless. Leslie does not create that intense feeling of concentration which most gymnasts exhibit when they pull off their beam routine. Instead, she brings a balletic, dancelike quality to her movements, shifting from one routine to another so smoothly that the audience hardly realizes what she has accomplished.

Leslie placed ninth among the thirty-eight top female gymnasts in the country who were competing in the Princeton meet. She received a 9.55, among the highest scores in the entire competition, for her uneven bars routine.

"When I do well," says Leslie, "it gives me fantastic joy."

As a result of excelling in Princeton, the Foreign Relations Committee of the United States Gymnastics Federation selected Leslie as one of three American girls to represent the United States in a gymnastics competition in Capetown, South Africa in the spring. She was chosen on the basis of being recognized as an "outstanding newcomer to Elite gymnastics."

By being selected for this competition, it was a clear sign to everyone in the gymnastics world that Leslie was being groomed for top international competition, such as the 1978 World Games and the 1980 Olympics. Don Peters was selected as the U.S. coach to accompany the girls, so Leslie had the good fortune of traveling with her own tutor.

South Africa provided an uneasy introduction to international competition. Leslie was now competing against gymnasts from Sweden, Switzerland, West Germany, Japan, Norway, and Taiwan. "I had just gotten used to competing against people like Kolleen Casey," says Leslie. "Now I was competing against people I couldn't even talk to because they didn't speak English. It was weird."

Despite the fact that she felt like a novice, Leslie captured top honors. She competed in three meets, including the prestigious Sanlan Cup, and won three gold medals and three bronze medals.

"Leslie is more of a little jock than everybody imagines," says Muriel. "She enjoys the act of physicality. But she has no killer instinct. I don't know how Leslie would do in a team sport or, say, in boxing, where you have to eliminate the other person. But in gymnastics the competition is between her and the piece of apparatus. She gets a number [a score] for it and if that number holds, fine."

During her month's stay in South Africa, Leslie put on a hard hat and goggles, descended over two miles into a diamond mine and watched the diamond cutters at work. She bought a small diamond as a present for her mother's twenty-fifth wedding anniversary. With the other gymnasts she did handstands on the roof of their hotel in Capetown. She took a bus to the hinterland to see the wild animals that crowded around the vehicle, and when she wasn't rushing around, she got homesick. She called her parents in Connecticut. It cost $92 for the first three minutes.

Now when Leslie goes on a long trip, her mother says, "Don't call. Write!"

The following October, 1977, Leslie was picked as the only American representative from the United States for the prestigious Barcelona International Gymnastics Competition. Even though ten nations were represented, the competition turned out to be a battle between the Soviet and American entries. In the women's competition, Leslie placed second in the All-Around to the Soviet entry Galina Gluschenco, also age fourteen.

With American gymnast Kurt Thomas

When Leslie received a call in November inviting her to represent the United States at the Tokyo International Elite Competition, called the Chunichi Cup, along with participants from the USSR, Romania, Japan, Hungary, Czechoslovakia, and East Germany, her first thoughts went to food. Somebody told her that the Japanese eat odd concoctions of snakes, eels, and turtles. Leslie was afraid that if she developed an upset stomach from Japanese meals she wouldn't be able to perform. So she packed a large box of saltine crackers and two kinds of Skippy peanut butter, crunchy and smooth, with her leotards. She also packed her stuffed walrus named Walry. "I take him to all the meets," she says. "He's sort of like a good luck charm."

There is a custom in gymnastics in which members of competing teams exchange leotards. "We trade them with everybody," says Leslie. "But in Japan a lot of the girls didn't speak English so we just pointed to each other and smiled."

For several months, Leslie had been working on a difficult trick, part of her floor exercise routine, a high-flying and smooth landing doubleback somersault, a feat that had never been accomplished by any American gymnast. "It took me about a year and a half of practice," says Leslie, "because I had to work on it every single day to get the feel of it. It takes about a month just to know where you are in the air. Because if you don't know, you'll land on your head. And if you go halfway, you can kill yourself because you won't make it all the way around."

At the Chunichi Cup Leslie pulled it off. She executed not only the doubleback somersault, but also a double twisting somersault, establishing herself as a World Class tumbler. Her routine scored 9.45 and earned her second place in the competition.

Leslie's teammate, Jackie Cassello, then eleven years old, had been working on the same trick in the gym. Jackie, a feisty contender, who had traveled alone from Kennedy Airport, via Washington, to the U.S.A.-Czechoslovakia Junior Competition in Albuquerque, New Mexico, which was taking place at the same time as the Chunichi Cup, was as determined as Leslie to be the first American to perform the doubleback somersault. She performed the trick about twelve hours later.

Muriel remembers. "She wanted to be first so bad you could see it all over her ears."

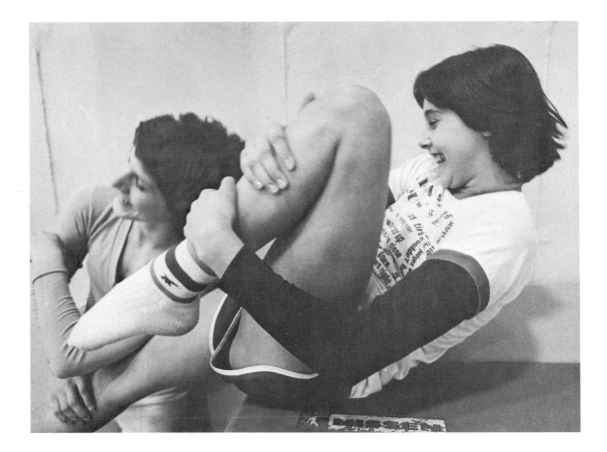

Leslie's magnificent skill, her innovation, her simplicity, and her personal charm made her the darling of the Japanese crowds, particularly Japanese boys. They lined up by the dozens outside her hotel room in Tokyo waiting to catch a glimpse of her. Even today, Leslie receives bundles of letters from her Japanese fans. They say things like "Dear Miss Leslie, I love you. You're so good at gymnastics. Please show us your elegant figure, forever, forever, forever...."

Jetting around the globe made Leslie a celebrity at Coginchaug High. It also set her apart from the other students. She didn't know how to handle that. "We'd be changing classes and one of my friends would come up to me and say, 'Hi, Sport,' 'Hi, Star,' or 'Leslie, can I have your autograph?' I said, 'You know me. You don't need my autograph.' Somebody else would come along and say, 'Hey, Les. You going anyplace international this month?'

"It makes me feel like a freak when people treat me like an actress or something. Actresses know everybody knows who they are and they act like it. But I'm a regular person, like my friend Karen next door. I don't feel any higher than her."

Leslie is now fifteen and each day she looks less like a child and more like a young woman. When she was younger, she used to just pull on her jeans and walk out the front door to school. Now she cares how she looks. "We have a big mirror in the bedroom," says Val. "She's in front of it every two minutes checking herself out." Leslie agrees: "I love clothes. I could spend ten hours in a shopping mall and not get bored."

Mrs. Russo began to suspect that Leslie had a secret boyfriend but the truth is she doesn't know any boys very well. "Some of the guys at school say they're afraid to ask me out because I'm a big star and they're nothing. I'd like to meet somebody who treats me like an average person. Somebody who's nice—and cute."

Just at the time when everything was going so well for her in gymnastics, Leslie developed health problems. In the months following her return from Japan, she had tendinitis in her finger, tonsilitis, and mononucleosis.

During that period, a representative of the Soviet Union called and invited her to come there for an exhibition match; the Rumanians called, and the Japanese invited her back to Japan. "I was sorry I told her about those invitations," Mrs. Russo says, "because she broke down and cried. But I figured, if she's going to be a champion, she's going to have to learn to lose."

Leslie couldn't go to the gym for twelve long weeks. "I just moped around the house," she remembers. "Did a lot of sleeping. I exercised to stay in shape but I felt real tired."

With her mother

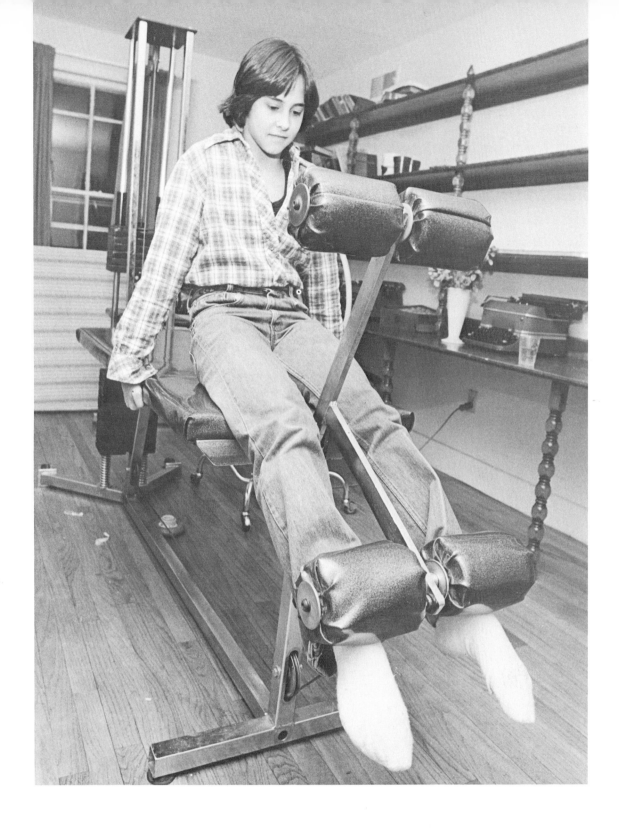

She was also depressed, which is not at all like Leslie. Depression is a frequent side effect of mononucleosis. No matter what anybody said to her, she couldn't climb out of the dumps. She waited by the phone, hoping her friends from the gym would call, which they often did.

The girls missed Leslie. She was not only a buddy but a leader.

For Jackie Cassello, Leslie was particularly important. Jackie had just arrived at Grossfeld's in 1977, loaded with talent, a tough competitor, but only eleven years old. She started hanging out with girls who weren't succeeding. She went in for too much horseplay in the dorm; she stayed up too late and then wasn't able to do well in workout because she was tired. Also, since Grossfeld's was Jackie's first long-term exposure to the big leagues, she had a lot to learn about techniques.

Jackie Cassello (center)

Nadia Comaneci

Leslie was a perfect example for Jackie of what kind of work needs to be done to be a top-level gymnast and how you should approach it. Jackie could take advice from Leslie because Leslie was a contemporary. Also, Leslie provided Jackie with stimulating rivalry. "She's still a kid," says Leslie. "When she misses, she starts crying. Not real bad but she just gets a face on her. Her eyes water. But then she gets up and tries to do it until she makes it."

Jackie is from South Hempstead, Long Island. She is the best young gymnast in her age group in the country and she earned a berth on the Junior National Team when she was only ten.

Like Leslie, Jackie was introduced to the world of competitive gymnastics through television. Her idol was Nadia Comaneci, the star of the 1976 Montreal Olympics. Jackie sat glued to the Cassellos' color TV on Locust Street watching Nadia achieve the "impossible"—seven 10.00 scores—more perfect scores than anyone in gymnastics. She jumped up and shouted, "I can do that! I'm going to be as good as Nadia, maybe even better."

While Leslie's self-confidence was built up slowly, Jackie always thought of herself as a winner. "Jackie is the sort of person who thrives on the idea of competition," explains Muriel. "She can't wait to get out on the floor. In her mind she's thinking, 'How good I am.' She doesn't worry about thinking she's bad."

Even as a little girl, Jackie knew her own mind. When she was four, she made her own breakfast. "She was like a little old lady," remembers Mrs. Cassello. "I could trust her to go to the store for me and never get anything wrong. She was very responsible. I think you have to be responsible to be a gymnast. You have to be very disciplined."

Now Jackie is on the verge of adolescence, aggressive, exciting, and bubbling all the time. She is the exact opposite of what Leslie was like at that age. If Jackie visits a friend's home, she digs right in by answering the phone, putting the dishes away, and feeding the dog. She's like a little clockwork doll. She's wound up all the time and then, when she gets tired, she just goes plop.

Jackie started to compete in local meets when she was nine. For a natural gymnast like Jackie, the competition was not stiff. "Some of the kids would run out to the middle of the auditorium to do their floor exercise and they would forget their routine and walk off."

Jackie trained at Schnaar's Gym, near her home, after school and at a gymnastics camp in the summer. "She could never get enough of gymnastics," says Nancy Lauster, her coach at camp. "She always wanted more practice time. When they love it that much, you know they've got what it takes to be a champ."

But Jackie's life was not easy and at times it was very lonely. She was "different" in her grade school because she had no time to spend with other kids after school. It was hard for her to make friends when every day she had to rush home to get ready for gym. "The kids would say to me, 'Can't you miss gym this one night and come to our party?'" Jackie always said no, but she didn't like being made to feel odd. And she didn't really fit in at the gym because she was so much better than the other students, she had to be coached alone. "I'd be at the gym and I'd say to myself, 'What am I doing here? Why do I come? I don't know why I like it so much.'"

Because she had few friends, Jackie relaxed mostly by herself. She listened to pop records and she painted.

When the Cassellos decided to send Jackie to live at the Grossfeld's Gymnastics Center, she couldn't wait to go.

"She's only two hours away and she comes home for weekends," says Mrs. Cassello. "So she hasn't really lost her family. She has her friends at the school and she still has us. She has a bigger family now."

Indeed she has. Jackie's roommates come from several eastern states: Massachusetts, Pennsylvania, New York, and Connecticut. The girls at the dorm think of each other as sisters. There they find the usual mix of jealousies, fights, making up, sharing, and loving.

The rules at the dorm are strict. The girls are assigned chores around the house, such as vacuuming or cleaning the bathrooms. Each girl does her own laundry and is responsible for cooking her own dinner. They tried a communal dining table but the girls put on too much weight. Every gymnast at Grossfeld's is on a diet. Extra weight saps strength and the gymnast does not look as elegant when she performs.

Jackie is now a chef, broiling steaks, cooking lamb chops, fried chicken, and mashed potatoes. She bakes a cake whenever somebody has a birthday.

Most of the girls buy their groceries when they go home on weekends or they go shopping with the help of the dorm parents. Everybody's supplies are stored in the same refrigerator.

Sometimes, on a Saturday noon when the girls get tired of cooking, some of them will sneak down the backstairs and over to Burger King, a mile or so away, for a Double-Cheeseburger, fries, and a shake. "If a dorm parent notices that a couple of kids are missing, we'll stick up for them," says Jackie. "We'll say they're in the bathroom."

The girls work out after school six hours every day five days a week unless they are sick or taking exams. They may go home on the weekends, and they take brief vacations during the year, a week around the Fourth of July and a week at Christmas.

But Jackie soon found that the steady training schedule was balanced with fun. "In the summer, Muriel takes us sailing, motorboat riding—whatever happens to be going on," says Jackie. "We've gone to an amusement park, a haunted house, and a bagel factory. And when there's nothing else to do, we can always go over to Muriel's house and play pool."

Since coming to Grossfeld's, Jackie has taken up fishing. She carries her Olympic Silver Spinner rod and her tackle box down to the beach near Muriel's house out on Long Island Sound, and sits with the other fishermen, waiting for the baby blues to bite.

Jackie and the other girls who board at Grossfeld's attend Milford Academy, a private school to which each member of the elite team has been given a scholarship. Gymnasts tend to do better academically than most other students. If the Grossfeld girls don't do well they hear about it from Don, who goes over their report cards. "The better you are doing in gym, the better your grades get," says Jackie. "I don't know why. It just happens that way."

For many committed gymnasts, their worries are not about school, but about money. Most of the girls come from middle- to upper-income families, a few are rich and a few poor. At the Grossfeld Gymnastics Center there are the monthly costs for instruction, boarding, and expenses. Leotards can run as high as $250 to $300 a year. The Russos estimate that Leslie's gymnastics career has cost $7000 already.

The Russos pay Grossfeld's $100 a month for her training but that sum only accounts for about a sixth of the costs of training Leslie. The same is true for the other eleven gymnasts. The salaries of the coaches, the trips to competitions, and the maintenance of the building add up. In order to raise money, the staff at Grossfeld's pitches in with fund-raising projects, such as organizing gymnastics exhibitions in Connecticut and nearby areas.

Some girls are also partially financed by sponsors. Often, if the family of a talented gymnast can't pay for their daughter's instruction, civic organizations in her hometown, such as the Elks, the Rotarians, or the Girl Scouts, will sponsor fund-raising events. Usually the girl has made a name for herself as a gymnast in her local area. If she doesn't immediately produce medals when she goes into training, her sponsors may be disappointed. The added pressure of being up against top competitors for the first time and unable to explain the situation adequately to the sponsors causes some girls to buckle and they cannot perform well.

Jackie Cassello is one of the twenty-one girls in the United States under the age of fourteen who is actively training for the 1980 Olympics. Because the United States has never done well in major international gymnastics competitions, in 1977, officials of the USGF decided to establish a program geared to athletically gifted children. "Our first goal was to identify the outstanding kids," says Frank Bare, executive director of the USGF. After a nationwide talent search, the girls were chosen for the Junior Elite Squad. They get together four times a year at week-long training camps, and they are invited to appear at special exhibitions. As part of the program, Jackie was chosen to perform in exhibition at Madison Square Garden in the spring of 1978.

"I got so tired of signing autographs," says Jackie, "that I thought my hand was going to fall off."

How did sixty-five-pound Jackie feel about performing before thousands of people in places like Madison Square Garden? "I was scared at first, but then I realized it's not so different from being at practice," she says. "I just feel like trying harder when there are people watching."

For Jackie, the biggest thrill of her life was when the Rumanian national team came to the United States in November, 1977 and, as a Junior Elite, she was chosen to appear with them in an exhibition tour. This meant she could finally meet her idol, Nadia Comaneci.

Nadia, who speaks English, was friendly to Jackie. Sweets are taboo for Nadia, as they are for her American counterparts. Her coach keeps a close eye on her but the lure of American junk food shattered Nadia's resolve. One day Nadia slipped Jackie a twenty dollar bill and whispered, "Chocolates, doughnuts, cokes, candy bars..."

Nadia's request is not uncommon. Junk food is a strong bond between American and Soviet athletes. At the Chunichi Cup competition in 1973, American gymnast Joan Rice lowered Coca-Cola bottles on ropes from her hotel window to Ludmila Tourischeva, two floors below.

When Leslie returned to the gym after her bout with mononucleosis, Don and Muriel told her that she would not be strong enough to compete in the upcoming National Championships for 1978 at Long Island's Nassau Coliseum. This meant she would miss the most important women's gymnastics meet in the United States. In her mind, Leslie had been working up to this competition for a long time.

For this meet, Muriel's and Don's attention focused on Marcia Frederick, an introspective, shy person until she puts on a leotard. Marcia is Leslie's friend and chief competitor at Grossfeld's Gym. Gymnastics is Marcia Frederick's world. In this world she spends most of her time. It is here she builds her confidence.

Marcia is continually fascinated by the uneven bars. "I was nine when I started," she says. "The uneven bars has always been my best event. But I really began to get good last year when I came to Muriel's."

Just as Olga Korbut was Leslie's heroine and Nadia Comaneci spurred Jackie on, Muriel Grossfeld is the person Marcia admires most. When she first arrived at the gym, Marcia wanted to earn Muriel's respect. Now she wants to be like her.

Six girls from Grossfeld's were competing in the National Championships, but the entire team traveled in a caravan of cars to the competition on Long Island, so that the up-and-coming contenders could become acclimated to high-level competition.

World Games gold medalist Marcia Frederick (extreme right)

The girls stay four to a room in the hotel at meets away from home. Muriel does not permit the parents to stay at the same hotel for fear that they might make her students nervous.

"Next to winning, I like the trips best," says Leslie, who remained cheerful during the Nassau Championships despite the fact that she was not a contestant.

Instead of sulking over the fact that she couldn't compete, Leslie volunteered to be the team manager. She walked onto the competitive floor at the Coliseum right behind Muriel and Don and she helped out whenever she could. If a girl needed a comb or a Coke, Leslie got it. When Muriel had trouble getting Marcia to concentrate, Leslie reassured Marcia that she would "hit" all her tricks.

"Leslie offers quiet and continuous support," says Muriel. "She's not the kind to slap a kid on the back and say, 'Hey. Do good,' and then walk away. She will put her arm around you for a couple of seconds and sort of just stay there."

Just before the competition started, Muriel gathered her six protégées about her and gave them a final pep talk. "I know you guys can do it. I know you can win this meet. Just hit your routines the way you do in practice. Show them that short people are elite."

The girls were facing the toughest competition in the United States. Kathy Johnson, who won the American Cup Competition in 1977 and was named U.S. Female Gymnast of the Year, was there. Kathy, who is eighteen and a perfectly constituted ninety-four pounds, has become one of the world's best performers and a potential winner in the 1980 Olympics. She has more experience and poise than the younger girls.

"She's sophisticated," observed Marcia. "She's been in hard competition for two years. She's been in big meets. She knows how to compete; how to pace herself."

When Marcia's turn came to do the uneven bars there was a low buzz in the audience because a lot of people knew that Marcia is tops.

Sitting on the sidelines, Leslie watched Marcia advance toward the bars. She admires Marcia's excellence, enjoys the thrill of watching her but hates to be a spectator and not a participant.

"Come on, Marsh," Leslie shouted, blowing big pink bubble gum balloons. Then she parked her gum in one side of her mouth, stuck two fingers in her mouth and gave a loud, high whistle.

In a split second, Marcia flew up to the upper bar, touched it gently with her hands, and standing bent over, began to fall.

In bars, the concept of swing is very important. When you swing, the farther away you are from the rail you are swinging from, the longer the arc of the swing is. Marcia swings more freely and farther away from the bar than any woman gymnast competing today. The upper rail is thick, and when she goes to swing across the bottom not much is left of her hand on top. She is hanging on by the last eighth of an inch of skin at the end of her fingertips. Yet, she must hold on because the bottom of the swing has great gravitational force. She is willing to do that, to commit herself to such reckless abandon.

Marcia did a one-and-a-half twist, hit her stomach on the low bar and did another full twist-swing in the air. She finished her routine with a high front somersault, spinning, turning, and twisting.

It was a magnificent performance.

"Mmmm, that's good," murmured Leslie, tears of admiration welling up in her eyes.

Marcia Frederick (right)

"A ten for Marcia Frederick," said the announcer.

The crowd went wild, yelling and whistling and clapping. Television cameras dollied in. Reporters and photographers swarmed around her. In the midst of the cyclone, Leslie stood talking to Marcia, praising her, going over the high points of the routine.

At the closing ceremonies the gymnasts marched around the auditorium, each carrying a bouquet of roses. They were supposed to toss their flowers to the crowd. Marcia threw a couple of roses, but she guarded her bouquet, and when she marched past her mother, who was sitting in a front-row seat, she moved toward her and handed her the flowers. "Here Mommy," she said, "These are for you."

Leslie and Marcia are both fifteen and that's not young in gymnastics. While it's true that the 1977 Chunichi Cup had a 35-year-old woman competitor, the hot gymnasts coming out of the Soviet Union, the United States and Canada are only eleven, twelve and thirteen years old. "In this sport, sixteen can be ancient," says Muriel.

Older girls used to dominate the sport but ever since the Soviets captured the limelight, the judges have favored the younger gymnasts. "World-Class gymnasts usually begin their careers while they still have their baby teeth," said sports writer Gerald Eskenazi in *The New York Times.* Physically, the little ones have the advantage—their pelvises are narrower, which gives them an advantage in running and twisting. They recover quickly from sore muscles. They are extremely flexible, especially in the back, and many of them attempt stunts requiring extraordinary courage.

Gymnasts are constantly fighting physical and mental fatigue. They often drop out very young in this sport. "People are afraid they'll peak," says Leslie. "They think they are going to start going downhill so they quit while they are ahead."

After her bout with mononucleosis, Leslie thought she had put bad luck behind her, but when she returned to workouts she began to feel pain. "I could feel a sore spot in my lower back and it got worse and worse." She tried to ingore it but the pain didn't go away. Dr. Anthony Sterling, the team doctor, said her pelvis was inflamed. Gymnastics is especially hard on young bones. He told her to lie on her back for two weeks, until the inflammation went down.

Since Leslie had become totally disciplined and completely committed to the sport, she was faced with a setback that could put an end to her career.

Leslie knew that back injuries can be serious. During her recuperation, she lay on the sofa in the Russos' family room reading a paperback biography of Olga Korbut. But she knew she was walking a thin, hard line between a championship and oblivion. If she wasn't lucky, she might go the way of young Stephanie Willim.

In 1977, at the age of twelve, Stephanie's name was known to everyone in the gymnastics world. She had experienced the success and excitement of foreign competition, her own fan club, TV and newspaper coverage. But, as her body grew, she started to feel pain in her back. A succession of orthopedic specialists who x-rayed her gave the same tragic answer: A weakness from birth had shown up and unless Stephanie retired from gymnastics she might suffer permanent injury. So, at the age of thirteen, she was forced to quit the sport.

Now, once again, Leslie is back at the gym, working out six hours a day, five days a week, pursuing her Olympic dream. But now she knows how fragile, how elusive that dream is; that Muriel and Don see many rising young stars come and go.

"I haven't known too many people who have risen to the top without some sort of setback," said Don Peters. "It's a timing thing. A lot can happen in two years. Right now, Leslie is one of the best up-and-coming competitors in the country."

Even if Leslie goes to the Olympics in Moscow in 1980, her career as a competitive gymnast will probably level off from there. "By twenty you're usually an old lady in this sport," said Muriel, "although that is not always the case. For some gymnasts, the maturity of movement, the precision, and accuracy improve greatly in their twenties."

Olga Korbut bowed out of competition when she was twenty-one and became a coach. Now Olga will be competing through her students and, she says, "It may be more frightening than performing myself—to watch the performance of someone I have trained and given my heart to."

Sitting around in Marcia's bedroom in the dorm one spring night, the "guys," as they call themselves, had a rap session, talking about their futures as adults after quitting competitive gymnastics.

Participation in elite gymnastics is a ticket to a college scholarship, as long as their marks are up to par. Many gymnasts, because they have supple acrobatic bodies, compete on college diving teams. Others go to Hollywood and become stunt performers in movies. While some of the women gymnasts choose to become housewives, a high percentage go into professions, working as lawyers, doctors, college professors, and bankers.

"Sometimes I think I want to be a coach," said Jackie. "It depends on how the kids are. I don't like to yell."

Marcia, an animal lover whose bedroom walls are plastered with posters of cats and dogs, said, "I'm planning to be a veterinarian."

"You mean you can't eat meat, Marsh?" asked Jackie.

"No. Stupid. That's a vegetarian!"

Leslie isn't sure what the future will bring for her. Her father has a dream of building a gymnastics school for Leslie. Leslie will coach and Val will teach dancing. But Leslie isn't thinking that far ahead. Her thoughts are still centered on a cushioned beam that could be her bridge to Moscow. Over and over again she does her flips, splits, and intricate ballet steps on the elevated layered beam, reciting to herself over and over again, "I want to be number one in the world."

GLOSSARY

Amplitude—Making the most of every position and movement. The maximum possible extension in an upward and outward position.

Apparatus—The equipment used for gymnastics.

Cartwheel—A smooth turning of the body sideways with the arms and legs functioning as the spokes of a wheel.

Cast—Pushing or thrusting the body away from the point of support while performing on the parallel bars.

Chalk—Magnesium carbonate. Using it on the hands before an event helps to prevent slipping due to sweat. Chalk is also applied to bars. It insures a firm, secure grip on the apparatus.

Compulsories—Each competitor must perform the routine precisely as set forth in the text. The highest scores are given for excellence of technique and form, rhythm, precision, lightness, elegance, and outstanding amplitude of movement.

Crash pad—Large, thick, soft mats, which provide a safe landing area if a movement goes wrong.

Dismount—The final movement in a routine, in which the gymnast goes from the uneven bars or balance beam to the floor.

Elite gymnast—A gymnast who is recognized as an international competitor.

Mount—The method used for getting up onto the uneven bars or balance beam.

Optionals—Each gymnast designs her routine on each event to enhance her best qualities. A routine must meet international requirements as to types and variety of movements and numbers of difficulties, but the selection of specific skills and their placement within the composition is done by the gymnast and her coach.

Pike—A position in which the body is bent forward at the hips while the legs are kept perfectly straight.

Qualifying meets—Meets among gymnasts or countries to establish who gets to compete at a major event.

Reuther board—The takeoff board used for vaulting and performing mounts on uneven bars. It is slightly inclined to aid in changing forward momentum to upward momentum. Also called a beat board.

Routine—A set of gymnastics skills performed on one event.

Safety belt—The belt used for learning new stunts, supports the gymnast in the air. It permits the gymnast to twist and turn by means of ropes and pulleys hung from the ceiling and attached around the performer's waist.

Trick—A movement or gymnastic skill.

Tuck—A position in which the knees are bent, the body is curved like a ball, and the legs are held tightly against the chest.

USGF—United States Gymnastics Federation. The governing body for gymnastics in the United States.

World Games—or *World Championships*—Competition between the nations of the world. Held between the Olympic years.

SCORING

BEGINNING with a perfect score of 10.0 points, the judges allot a maximum score of 3.0 points for difficulty, 1.5 points for originality, .5 points for composition, 4.0 points for execution and amplitude, and 1.0 point for general impression. Deduct .1 to .5 if the gymnast doesn't point her toes or if she bends her knees awkwardly, bends elbows, interrupts her rhythm, stops short, or takes small steps after dismounting. If she stumbles on landing, touches the floor, or fails to complete a move, another .3 to .8 points are deducted. If a gymnast falls from the apparatus, fails to complete her routine, falls on landing, skips a part, or performs without energy or rhythm, then .5 to 1.0 are deducted.

Four judges score each performance. Each of the judges presents her score to the head judge independently of one another. Among the scores obtained for each competitor, the highest and lowest scores are eliminated and the middle scores are averaged.

The all-around score is the total of the points earned on all events. The highest possible score in each event is 10.00 points; therefore, the all-around total is 40.00 points. Since most international competitions require a set of compulsory routines as well as a set of optional routines, the number of possible points is actually doubled to 80.00 points.

2038